WHAT WE GET FROM ROMAN MYTHOLOGY

MARGARET MINCKS

Published in the United States of America
by Cherry Lake Publishing
Ann Arbor, Michigan
www.cherrylakepublishing.com

Consultants: Thomas Keith, Instructor, Liberal Arts, School of the Art Institute of Chicago; Marla Conn, ReadAbility, Inc.
Editorial direction and book production: Red Line Editorial

Photo Credits: Shutterstock Images, cover, 1, 15, 22 (right); Viacheslav Lopatin/Shutterstock Images, 5; Richard T. Nowitz/Corbis, 7; Bettmann/Corbis, 9; Corbis, 11; Georgios Kollidas/Shutterstock Images, 16; Edwin Henry Landseer, 18; Titian, 21; Claudio Giovanni Colombo/Shutterstock Images, 22 (left); Paramount/Everett Collection, 27, 29 (bottom); Paul Fell/Shutterstock Images, 29 (top); Galushko Sergey/Shutterstock Images, 29 (center)

Library of Congress Cataloging-in-Publication Data

Mincks, Margaret, author.
  What we get from Roman mythology / by Margaret Mincks.
    pages cm. -- (Mythology and culture)
  Includes index.
  ISBN 978-1-63188-915-8 (hardcover : alk. paper) -- ISBN 978-1-63188-931-8 (pbk. : alk. paper) -- ISBN 978-1-63188-947-9
(pdf) -- ISBN 978-1-63188-963-9 (hosted ebook)
  1. Mythology, Roman--Juvenile literature. 2. Civilization--Roman influences--Juvenile literature. 3. Rome--Civilization-
-Juvenile literature. I. Title.

  BL803.M56 2015
  398.20937--dc23

                    2014029974

Cherry Lake Publishing would like to acknowledge the work of
The Partnership for 21st Century Skills. Please visit www.p21.org
for more information.

Printed in the United States of America
Corporate Graphics
December 2014

ABOUT THE AUTHOR

Margaret Mincks lives in Windermere, Florida, with her husband Scott and their dog, Reesie.
Her favorite book of Roman mythology is Ovid's *Metamorphoses*.

TABLE OF CONTENTS

Roman Religion

In ancient Rome, religion was a part of everyday life. Romans spoke Latin, and the Latin word *religio* means "something that binds." For Romans, religion united families. It also connected citizens to their leaders and their gods. Roman religion was divided into two parts. The first was private worship in households. The second was public worship in state temples.

The early Romans worshiped many gods and spirits. These gods and spirits were called numina, or **divine** powers. Citizens performed daily **rituals** for these numina. They asked the spirits to protect their harvests, keep them safe from danger, and help them in other ways.

Over time, Rome grew from a small farming village to a powerful empire. Roman armies conquered

The Temple of Venus, one of ancient Rome's largest temples, stands in the middle of Rome today.

surrounding lands. The Roman people began borrowing religious beliefs and stories from other cultures. They especially admired the Greeks, who were known for brilliant art, science, and storytelling.

In the second and first centuries BCE, the Romans faced troubled times. They fought many wars. Then, in 44 BCE, a group of Roman politicians killed their own leader, Julius Caesar.

Augustus, Julius Caesar's great-nephew, restored peace in Rome. Augustus was the first Roman emperor. He became a hero to the Roman people. Augustus expanded the Roman Empire. He also brought back old social rules and religious rituals.

Many great Roman **myths** were created during Augustus's rule. This **mythology** was often about the history, founding, and heroes of Rome. To Romans, loyalty to Rome was important. Stories of duty, heroism, and honor inspired citizens to put Rome above themselves.

LOOK AGAIN

THIS ROMAN COIN FEATURES AN IMAGE OF AUGUSTUS.
HOW IS THIS COIN LIKE THE COINS WE USE TODAY?
WHAT CAN YOU LEARN FROM THIS PICTURE ABOUT HOW
ROMANS THOUGHT OF THEIR LEADERS?

Roman Gods and Goddesses

Roman gods were similar to Greek gods, but they were not identical. Mars was the Roman version of the Greek god of war, Ares. The Greeks feared Ares's violent temper. For them, he represented the chaos and horror of war. The Romans admired Mars for his courage and military skill. They also believed he helped ensure the growth of their crops.

The most important Roman gods were Jupiter, Juno, and Minerva. They formed a family. Jupiter, the god of the sky, ruled over the other gods. The solar system's

Mars is often shown as a warrior.

largest planet is named after him. Juno, his wife, was the goddess of childbirth and marriage. Ancient Romans believed she protected Rome. Minerva, Jupiter's daughter, represented education and the arts, among other things. Like Mars, she was also associated with war.

Romans also worshiped gods from other cultures in Italy. One was Janus, the god of doors and beginnings. He was depicted as a two-faced god, looking forward and backward. Janus is known for his connection to Rome's wars. During peacetime, the gates of the Temple of Janus in Rome were closed. But during war, the authorities opened them. The temple doors remained open most of the time.

The Romans believed the gods were involved in the creation of Rome. They felt this meant the gods were on their side. They believed the goddess Venus was the mother of Aeneas, the father of the Roman people. Mars was the father of Romulus, who founded the city of Rome. Romans felt deep connections between Rome, the gods, and war.

The warrior Aeneas is the mythological hero of the *Aeneid,* an epic poem written by the Roman poet Virgil in 19 BCE. Aeneas is shown as being responsible for Rome's **origins**. In the *Aeneid,* the god Apollo tells Aeneas to go to Italy. Aeneas makes many sacrifices to fulfill his destiny. He leaves behind his home and the people he loves. Aeneas embarks on a long, dangerous journey away from Troy, in present-day Turkey. He reaches Italy, where his descendants later establish

In the Aeneid, *Aeneas voyages throughout the Mediterranean region.*

Rome. Aeneas represents the qualities that Romans valued most. These include honor, bravery, and duty.

Romulus and Remus, sons of the god Mars, were mythical twin brothers related to Aeneas. They lived many generations after him. As babies, the twins were left to die but were rescued by a wolf. Later, a shepherd found them and raised them.

When the twins grew up, they wanted to create their own city. They argued over who would be king. A fight broke out, and Romulus killed Remus. Romulus became the ruler of the new city. He named it Rome after himself. He became the first of the seven kings of Rome.

Another popular work that tells of Roman mythology is the *Metamorphoses*. The *Metamorphoses* is a collection of more than 200 myths gathered by the Roman poet Ovid in 8 CE. The word *metamorphoses* means "transformations." Some of the most famous Roman myths come from this collection.

Transformation is the main theme of the *Metamorphoses*. Ovid retold many Greek myths for Roman audiences. In doing so, he helped transform them into part of Roman mythology. The best-known versions of these myths survive today through Ovid's colorful retellings. In one Greek story Ovid retold, a sculptor named Pygmalion falls in love with his creation. The goddess Venus brings the statue to life. In another, a woman named Arachne challenges the goddess Minerva to a weaving contest. Minerva then turns Arachne into a spider. King Midas is another character in the *Metamorphoses*. He suffers from a curse during which everything he touches turns to gold, including the food he tries to eat. He is also given donkey ears for offending the god Apollo. One of the most popular myths is about the doomed young lovers Pyramus and Thisbe. Ovid and his stories frequently appear in later versions of Roman myths.

GO DEEPER

WHY DID THE ROMANS THINK SO HIGHLY OF WAR? FIND EVIDENCE FROM CHAPTER ONE AND CHAPTER TWO TO SUPPORT YOUR CLAIMS.

CULTURAL LEGACY

In the 300s CE, Christianity became the official religion of the Roman Empire. Worship of Roman gods was forbidden. By 476, the Western Roman Empire had fallen. It was replaced by the kingdoms of **medieval** Europe.

Although Roman mythology lost its religious significance, many parts of it survived. The myths were retold through the **Middle Ages**, the **Renaissance**, and beyond. The Middle Ages lasted from the 400s until the 1400s. The Renaissance lasted from the end of the

Constantine, Rome's first Christian emperor, ruled in the early 300s.

Middle Ages until the 1600s. Some stories have had an especially strong influence on modern cultures.

The importance of the hero Aeneas to ancient Rome inspired later writers. Aeneas is mentioned in several works of medieval English literature. In the 1100s, British author Geoffrey of Monmouth claimed Aeneas was related to Brutus of Troy, the legendary founder of Britain. At the same time, Britons looked down on Aeneas because he abandoned his home in Troy. Scholars believe Aeneas is the true identity of a traitor

Dante incorporated ancient characters and historical figures into his Divine Comedy.

mentioned in the introduction to *Sir Gawain and the Green Knight*, a British legend from the late 1300s.

In medieval Italy, the poet Dante Alighieri was inspired by Aeneas. Aeneas, Virgil, and Ovid are all characters in Dante's epic poem the *Divine Comedy*, written in the 1300s. The *Divine Comedy* is divided into three parts, all of which deal with the Christian afterlife.

Part of the poem takes place in the Underworld, the land of the dead. Aeneas, Virgil, and Ovid cannot enter paradise because they believe in Roman mythology. However, the narrator still considers them **virtuous**.

Romulus was generally viewed in a negative light during the Middle Ages and the Renaissance. In the early Middle Ages, the Christian philosopher Saint Augustine used Romulus's murder of Remus as an example of evil. Centuries later, in Edmund Spenser's 1590 poem *The Faerie Queene*, Romulus is sent to Hell. He serves as a symbol of selfish pride that can destroy nations.

The *Metamorphoses* inspired Geoffrey Chaucer's *The Canterbury Tales*, written in the late 1300s. Chaucer's collection of loosely connected stories features many characters from Ovid's work. *The Canterbury Tales* is considered one of the greatest works of medieval literature.

The character Bottom has his head transformed into that of a donkey in A Midsummer Night's Dream.

English writers, such as the playwright William Shakespeare, used Ovid's myths in order to tell stories. Shakespeare's comic play *A Midsummer Night's Dream*, written in the 1590s, featured many of these references.

Characters within the play perform Ovid's Pyramus and Thisbe myth. At one point, an actor's head is transformed into a donkey's head. This refers to the King Midas myth.

The **legacy** of the *Metamorphoses* continued for centuries. Ovid's Pygmalion myth was the inspiration for George Bernard Shaw's 1912 play *Pygmalion*. In Shaw's version, the myth takes place in London in the early 1900s. *Pygmalion* was later adapted into the famous 1956 musical *My Fair Lady*.

THINK ABOUT IT
WHY DO YOU THINK ROMAN MYTHOLOGY INSPIRED LATER AUTHORS, POETS, AND PLAYWRIGHTS? WHY HAVE SOME OF ITS THEMES REMAINED POPULAR FOR SO LONG?

CHAPTER 4

Art and Language

Roman mythology has inspired artists and musicians as well as poets, playwrights, and philosophers. In ancient Rome, art was a way to show devotion. Artists created statues, carved temple walls, and painted divine images to honor the gods. In medieval times, Christian images replaced Roman gods and goddesses in art.

The Renaissance was a time of renewed interest in classical mythology. During this era, artists brought images from mythology into their work. One of the most famous paintings from the Renaissance is

The Birth of Venus by the Italian painter Sandro Botticelli. The artist Titian showed scenes from the *Metamorphoses* in his paintings.

Titian's The Death of Actaeon *shows a story from the* Metamorphoses.

LOOK AGAIN

Look at these photos of a Roman temple, left, and the U.S. Capitol building, right. What similarities can you see? Why might the builders of the U.S. Capitol have wanted to mirror architecture from ancient Roman religious buildings?

[21ST CENTURY SKILLS LIBRARY]

Roman mythology continued to inspire artists long after the Renaissance. In the 1800s, the English artist J. M. W. Turner painted scenes from the *Aeneid*. In the 1900s, modern artists such as Salvador Dali used Roman myths for inspiration.

Western musical composers have also been inspired by Roman mythology. The Aeneas myth was retold in the opera *Dido and Aeneas,* composed by Englishman Henry Purcell in 1689. It also appeared in the opera *The Trojans,* composed by Frenchman Hector Berlioz in 1856.

The English language contains countless references to Roman mythology. Roman names and stories live on through our planets, calendars, gardens, and everyday words.

Six of the eight planets in our solar system are named after Roman gods. They are Mercury, Venus, Jupiter, Mars, Saturn, and Neptune. Mars, known since ancient times, may have been named for its red color, which was associated with blood and war. Many moons, asteroids, and constellations are also named after Roman gods.

Several months are named after Roman gods. January is named for Janus. March is named for Mars. July and August are named for the emperors Julius Caesar and Augustus, both worshiped by the Romans. Saturday is named after Saturn, the Roman god of sowing and seed.

Terms in science and nature have also come from the Romans. The Venus flytrap plant is named after the goddess Venus. *Arachnid*, a scientific term for spiders, comes from Arachne. She became a spider in Ovid's *Metamorphoses*. The words *flora* and *fauna*, used to describe plant and animal life, come from the Roman gods Flora and Faunus.

One example of Roman mythology can be seen outside courthouses around the world. Many

Modern Words from Roman Mythology

FORTUNE	FROM FORTUNA, GODDESS OF FORTUNE
VOLCANO	FROM VULCAN, GOD OF FIRE
CEREAL	FROM CERES, GODDESS OF AGRICULTURE
JANITOR	FROM JANUS, GOD OF DOORS AND BEGINNINGS

courthouses feature a statue of a woman holding a set of balancing scales. She sometimes holds a sword as well. These statues of the Roman goddess Justitia represent the ideas of justice and fairness.

MYTHOLOGY IN MEDIA

Today, Roman mythology appears in many forms of media. Mythological stories, characters, and themes show up in books, television, movies, video games, and more.

Rick Riordan's 2011 book *The Son of Neptune* takes place at Camp Jupiter, a camp for Roman gods. It shows the Romans as more disciplined and warlike than the Greeks. In the Harry Potter books, Professor Minerva McGonagall is named after the Roman goddess

Minerva. Professor Remus John Lupin is named after Romulus's twin brother.

In the television and film franchise *Star Trek*, the names *Romulus* and *Remus* are used as the names of neighboring planets. The alien species known as the Romulans are enemies of another species called the Vulcans, who are named after the Roman god of fire.

Star Trek's *Romulans are aggressive and often at war.*

In Marvel comic books, Romulus is the name of an immortal wolf man. He causes trouble for the X-Men's Wolverine. Aeneas and several Roman gods also appear in Marvel comics.

Roman mythology often focused on war. Gods related to war were important to the Romans. Aeneas, the greatest Roman hero, was a mighty warrior. The gods' stories teach us what was important to the Romans. As the stories are retold in the present, they also reveal what matters to us today.

Roman stories and characters connect us to the past. They have inspired and entertained people for more than 2,000 years. Through literature, art, music, and language, Roman mythology lives on to inspire future generations.

LOOK AGAIN

LOOK AT THESE DEPICTIONS OF THE ROMAN GOD NEPTUNE FROM
DIFFERENT TIME PERIODS. HOW HAS PEOPLE'S IMAGE OF NEPTUNE
CHANGED OVER TIME?

THINK ABOUT IT

- In Chapter One, you learned that Rome fought many wars to become an empire. How do you think war affected the types of stories told in Roman mythology?

- One version of the Romulus and Remus myth says that Romulus did not kill his brother. Instead, it says that Remus was killed by Romulus's supporters. Does this version change your opinion of Romulus? Why or why not?

- The myths about Aeneas, Romulus, and Remus are stories about the beginnings of Rome. Why do you think these myths, also known as origin stories, were so important to the Romans?

[21ST CENTURY SKILLS LIBRARY]

LEARN MORE

FURTHER READING

James, Simon. *Ancient Rome*. New York: DK Children, 2008.

Lunge-Larson, Lise. *Gifts from the Gods: Ancient Words of Wisdom from Greek and Roman Mythology*. New York: Houghton Mifflin Harcourt, 2011.

Riordan, Rick. *The Son of Neptune*. New York: Disney/Hyperion Books, 2011.

WEB SITES

Encyclopedia Mythica
http://www.pantheon.org
This Web site includes information about all aspects of Roman mythology.

The Roman Empire in the First Century
http://www.pbs.org/empires/romans/empire/mythology.html
Visit this Web site to learn more about religion and many other elements of daily life in ancient Rome.

GLOSSARY

divine (duh-VINE) of, from, or like a god

legacy (LEG-uh-see) something handed down from the past

medieval (mee-DEE-vuhl) of or relating to the Middle Ages

Middle Ages (MID-uhl aje-is) a period in European history typically described as spanning the 400s to the 1400s

mythology (mi-THOL-uh-jee) a collection of myths dealing with a culture's gods or heroes

myths (MITHS) stories that attempt to describe the origin of a people's customs or beliefs or to explain mysterious events

origins (OR-uh-jinz) beginnings

Renaissance (REN-uh-sahnss) a period in European history after the Middle Ages, lasting until the 1600s

rituals (RICH-oo-uhlz) religious or solemn ceremonies performed according to a specific set of actions

virtuous (VUR-choo-us) having high moral standards

INDEX